SCHIRMER'S LIBRARY
OF MUSICAL CLASSICS

Vol. 1888

RICHARD STRAUSS

Concerto No. 1 in E-flat Major

Op. 11

For Horn and Piano

ISBN 0-7935-5007-6

G. SCHIRMER, Inc.

DISTRIBUTED BY

HAL•LEONARD®
CORPORATION
7777 W. BLUEMOUND RD. P.O. BOX 13819 MILWAUKEE, WI 53213

Printed in the U.S.A. by G. Schirmer, Inc.

Concerto No. 1 in E♭ Major

for horn and piano

Allegro. M. M. ♩=112.

Richard Strauss, Op. 11

Printed in the U.S.A. by G. Schirmer, Inc.

4

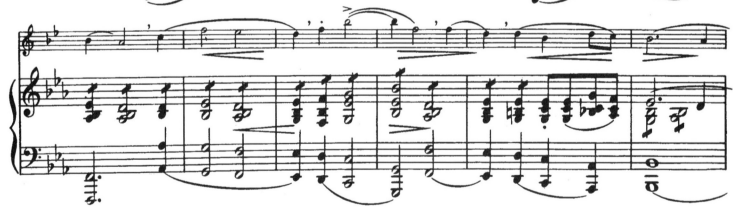

46992

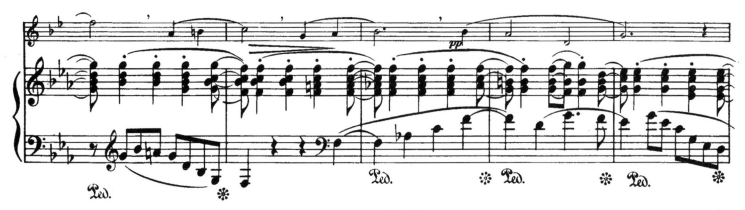

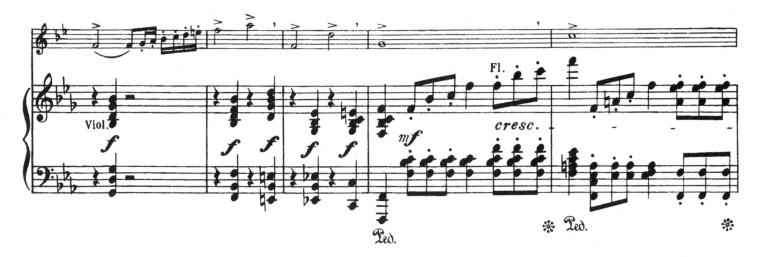

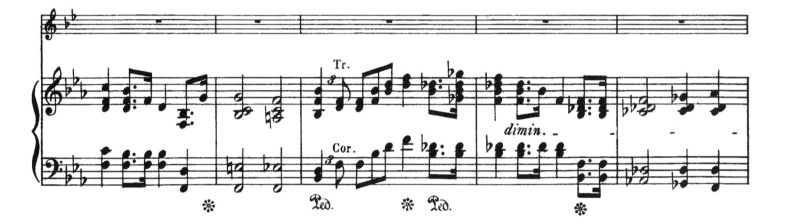

46992

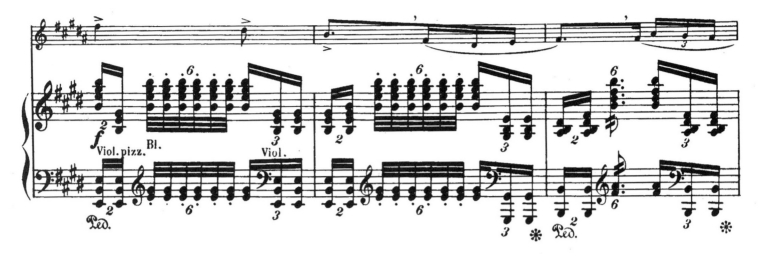

F Horn

F Horn

F Horn

F Horn

Concerto No. 1 in E♭ Major

for horn and piano

F Horn

Richard Strauss, Op. 11

Printed in the U.S.A. by G. Schirmer, Inc.

HORN in F

SCHIRMER'S LIBRARY
OF MUSICAL CLASSICS

Vol. 1888

RICHARD STRAUSS

Concerto No. 1 in E-flat Major

Op. 11

For Horn and Piano

ISBN 0-7935-5007-6

G. SCHIRMER, Inc.

DISTRIBUTED BY

HAL•LEONARD®
CORPORATION

7777 W. BLUEMOUND RD. P.O. BOX 13819 MILWAUKEE, WI 53213

Printed in the U.S.A. by G. Schirmer, Inc.

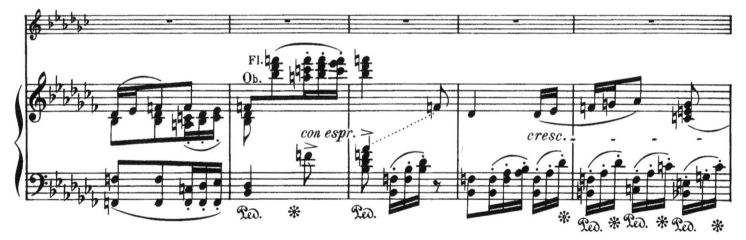

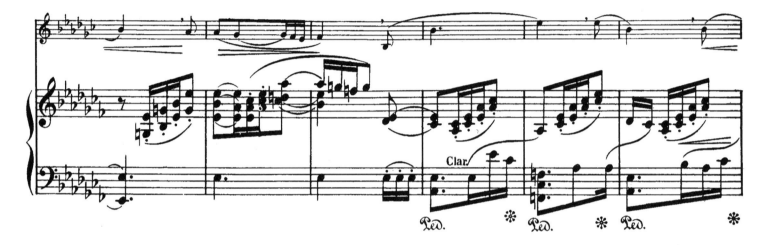

Tempo I.

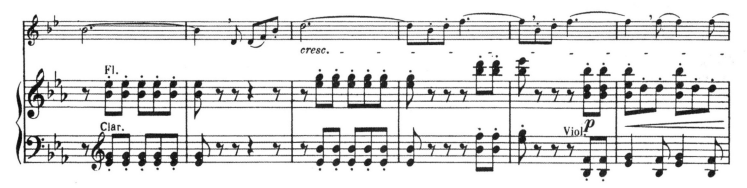